THE TIMES
WE LIVE IN

THE TIMES WE LIVE IN

JONATHAN CAPE
THIRTY BEDFORD SQUARE LONDON

First published 1978
© Mark Boxer and Lady Arabella Boxer 1978
Jonathan Cape Ltd, 30 Bedford Square, London WC1

British Library Cataloguing in Publication Data
Marc
The times we live in.
I. Title
741.5′942   NC1479.M28
ISBN 0-224-01654-7

Drawing of Tom Stoppard © 1977
The New Yorker Magazine, Inc.

Printed in Great Britain by
Ebenezer Baylis and Son Ltd
The Trinity Press, Worcester, and London

Introduction

If in the course of this introduction the reader gets the impression that I am looking over his shoulder all the time, like a social climber at a party keeping his eye on the new arrivals, I must apologise in advance. To tell the truth, it is not *you*, the contemporary reader, the astute purchaser of this valuable first edition, that I wish first and foremost to address. You are familiar enough, I think, with the context of most of these cartoons. Many of them have stuck in your mind through sheer force of merit, others because you cut them out and pinned them to your (O Tempora, O Shirley Conran!) kitchen notice-board, where they rapidly went yellow alongside the ('Oh my God, it's not our turn *again*?') residents' association duty rota, and others still because, every time you ran out of socks, you idly re-read the lining paper at the bottom of the drawer. The works of neglected poets were supposed to end up wrapping spices. *These* works, together with the uncollected thoughts of Bernard Levin, Alun Chalfont, Eric Heffer, Ronald Butt and PHS, as often as not ended up lining the garbage bin. How undignified they looked when the first tea-leaves began to fall. How right you were to make amends with this purchase.

But there—I am looking over your

shoulder again. It is not you whom I wish to
address. I am waiting for the next generation
to arrive. For the young visitor who, waking
in the early hours and regretting your
cooking, pulls this volume from the bedside
shelf. For the bookstall bargain-hunter, or
for Mr Maggs's future clientele ('Marc,
slightly foxed, only £10,000, 1st'). For
anyone who, though he will exclaim 'How
terribly Seventies', will know in his heart of
hearts that he does not know the first thing
he's talking about. Certainly it is difficult to
imagine the achievements of this decade
being engraved for ever on the minds of
future generations. What on earth have we
been up to all this time? Waging just wars?
Fostering the arts? Laying out magnificent
towns and parks? Or drinking far, far too
many of those two-litre bottles of Italian
wine? Certainly whole landscapes have been
dug up to accommodate our thirst, and the
vineyards of Tuscany, with their rows of
concrete poles, have come to look like vast
war cemeteries. As a typical invention of the
Age, I offer the hangover that begins with
the first sip from the glass.

The Age? Isn't that perhaps coming it a
bit strong? Isn't it a little early to be talking
of the Seventies, with the Sixties not yet cold
in their grave? Not yet, perhaps, in their
grave at all. The other day I breezed into
Cranks, off Carnaby Street, and was at once
transported into a different period: the
scraping of cutlery against rough stoneware,
the intelligent salads, the fruit juices, the

yoghurt culture ... It's nice, I thought, that it's still going on. Gradually, however, the full horror dawned on me. It was not still going on. It was being revived. I had walked into an event from the great Sixties revival. And logically, I realised, if one reaches the point where one revives yesterday, the next step is for Time to stop still altogether, leaving the customers at Cranks for ever ploughing through their mounds of grated carrot, their appetites for ever satisfied, for ever reviving, their watches for ever indicating that, yes, they have just enough time for a handful of nuts before sloping off to the Bonnard exhibition, with all that roughage envigorating their guts—a Dance to the Muesli of Time.

No, no—it must not be. Something must happen. Something must always shake us out of the mood. Gently or dramatically it must come. Like that sudden feeling that you never want to hear Scott Joplin again, or that the ear-ring was a mistake. So that one bravely decides: 'Now that I'm more or less completely bald, it's about time I started thinking bald.' Sometimes these decisions take a long time. Just as the new management of the Expresso Bongo, Station Road, is contemplating a new image, one may be certain that the programme planners at the B.B.C. are wondering whether it wouldn't be appropriate to revive *Expresso Bongo*. A company secretary said to me recently: 'We must give this magazine a relevance to the Seventies.' That, I reflected with some admiration and awe, was a thought of eight years' gestation.

If the Seventies may justly be called the Age of Revivals, it has been noteworthy that the supply of things to revive has dried up. Hence the dreary stalls at Camden Lock, piled high with tat. Hence the cult of junk. Hence the great queues of the middle classes at every jumble sale. Hence the second-hand clothes shops where vague young girls persuade vague young girls to buy foxes. Hence the fact that, whereas all over the rest of Europe children dress smartly, in London they look like the traditional Dutch boy in patched trousers. This affectation of poverty remains an affectation, even though it comes at a time when people have less money to throw around.

Poverty: it means such very different things to different people. To the characters in these cartoons one suspects that it involves a certain rearrangement of household expenditure and the novel experience of not being among the richest people in the world—the experience, above all, of making a great deal of money out of Arabs, *that's* poverty. It is the experience of the coloniser colonised, seeing Mayfair turned into a bazaar, Kensington snapped up, the country houses going under the hammer, and London turned into a fabulous international brothel. For that is what has happened, and it's mostly legal. The arriving Arab takes a double room in a luxury hotel, dials the head porter and orders a girl from an escort agency in precisely the same way as one would order a drink. In much the same way as a Westerner might behave in Bangkok. The hotel lobbies in London look just like hotels around the world, with the charming difference that the exotic characters swishing through are the clients rather than the staff. Viewed from the lower end of the social scale, these developments are not so bad: to the taxi-driver, whose business brings diminishing returns, the summer shortage of chauffeur-driven limousines presents quite an interesting job opportunity. On the other hand, the man who sells his house for a million is strangely reluctant to look on the bright side of the Arab invasion. It is an insult to his conception of caste.

The events of late 1973–4, the oil price rise, the miners' strike, the three-day week, form the watershed at least in our perception of the immediate past, if not in fact. Before then, the Heath Era—not so much an era as an aberration, an experiment in one form of radical Toryism: whizz-kids in the Government, whizz-kids in the City, the Barber boom based on 'the reckless printing of money to fuel the fires of future inflation' (a lot of f's in that phrase—an example of pure Seventies jargon). Afterwards, the return to Labour conservatism and the old familiar front bench. Before, the 'heroic, if misguided, attempt to curb the power of the unions'; after, the 'permanent incorporation of the unions in the decision-making process', and the discussion, although not the implementation, of 'legislation to give the worker a greater say in the management of his firm'. Afterwards also the rise of the neo-slob Tory, the man who sees that there is a lot to be said for the dictatorships, who considers Enoch Powell 'a thinker' of great profundity, whose aim is to put some real guts into Conservative ideology. Afterwards also the decline of the fellow-travelling Trot, the dispersal of the Class of '68 (followed inevitably by the tenth anniversary celebrations) and the rise of Eurocommunism as a theme for seminars. In a short while also came a complete turn-over in the leadership of the three main parties. In each case the circumstances were most peculiar, and the results profound.

* * *

Just how far can the art of the pocket cartoon be taken? Or is it an exaggeration even to think of it as an art? Certainly the rarity of good pocket cartoonists, like the scarcity of good political cartoonists, tells us something about the difficulty of the task. It is not enough to have a wry idea a day—even if this were easy. It is not nearly enough—although for many pocket cartoonists this seems to be the extent of their interest—to be able to draw two figures standing by a billboard, and tack on the wry idea underneath. The format is limited. The art consists in extending the range of suggestion beyond the physical space of the cartoon. The tell-tale detail, the happy choice

of facial type, the establishment of
continuity between one cartoon and the
next—all these are ways of reaching beyond
the boundaries of the individual drawing.
There must be a past, a future, an implicit
context—something happening off stage.

Can we guess, for instance, what the
husband of the lady searching for her signed
photograph of the King of Greece (July
1974) looks like? What their house looks
like? Who they are? And why on earth they
might come to possess a signed photograph
of the King of Greece? Can we guess what
frightful circumstances have led to Simon
Stringalong's slip of the tongue (February
1972)? Can we imagine the consequences? If
so, the cartoonist has achieved his aim of
providing, within a few square inches, what
the short story writer takes pages to relate.

Marc's cartoons are distinctive in this
respect. Taken together, they create a world
of comic types. Individually, they are
constantly suggestive of a particular place, a
particular moment, a particular facet of the
London they record. That frizzy-haired
young girl in the background, have we not
seen her in the Zanzibar? Do we not know
her voice, its harshness when roused, the
vigour of her argumentative style? Her
impatience in any world which she cannot
fully master—did this not strike us as both
admirable and cruel?

Or the lady with the head-scarf loosely
knotted on the strap of her handbag—is she
not precisely what cashmere was made to

contain? And is not her world, so well
serviced in all respects (with accounts at the
best stores, parking for residents alone, the
dark delivery vans shimmering in the heat),
precisely the part of London most threatened
in the last years? Threatened by burglars,
terrorists, the unions, taxes, the sinking
pound, the Arab colonist. No wonder so
many of these characters seem like members
of a threatened species. No wonder their
prime concern is survival.

N.W.1 is a haven of peace by comparison,
and might be accounted a desirable area were
it not for a certain thing that haunts its
inhabitants. The thing looks and behaves
very much like a conscience, but we have
known it long enough to be aware that it is
not in fact a conscience. Rather might it be
described as a general unease, nurtured and
developed by its sufferers over the years.
Look at the faces of the Stringalongs, his
furrowed brow and tense lips, her beady
eyes. How splendidly the unease has kept
them young and alert. It is as if they were
afraid that the *Zeitgeist* might pass them by,
like one of those rare night buses, leaving
them stranded in the suburbs of experience.

And yet even the Stringalongs have
developed a certain patina. Even they have a
past. Even *their* past has come to be revived.
Are they happy about this? Nobody likes to
be reminded of his age. And yet there is a
certain distinction in being revived. If the
Stringalongs never achieve anything else,
might they not finally settle for having been,

simply, the Stringalongs? And if the
Seventies never achieve anything else, might
they not settle for having been the Seventies?
Somebody had to get through the Seventies.
We did it, and surely now we deserve some
sort of reward. If there is nothing much for
which we can be remembered, we would
gladly be remembered, as here, for our
faults. Above all else, we should dearly like
to be revived.

Berlin   JAMES FENTON
July 1978

January 1971

‘And on the escritoire, pause to admire the exquisite richness of the cheque from Christies.

March 1971

July 1971

December 1971

18

Power strike
February 1972

Unpublished
February 1972

‘I have a feeling by the time the exhibition is over one may begin to wish the robbers had found the tomb after all,

March 1972

April 1972

Controversial royal portrait
at the Royal Academy
April 1972

'I think we have everything we need for this expedition, Carruthers: beads, mirrors, British passports...'

Asians with British passports
to be denied entry
August 1972

February 1973

July 1973

August 1973

Petrol shortage: coupons issued
December 1973

Uri Geller
December 1973

Mr Heath's three day week
December 1973

January 1974

February 1974

February 1974

March 1974

The Poulson affair
April 1974

6...and the weapon training will prepare you for civilian life,

May 1974

June 1974

June 1974

July 1974

The Greek colonels ousted
July 1974

August 1974

September 1974

The 'Siege' economy
October 1974

October 1974

November 1974

November 1974

November 1974

December 1974

December 1974

January 1975

February 1975

52

March 1975

March 1975

April 1975

April 1975

May 1975

58

May 1975

July 1975

July 1975

September 1975

October 1975

December 1975

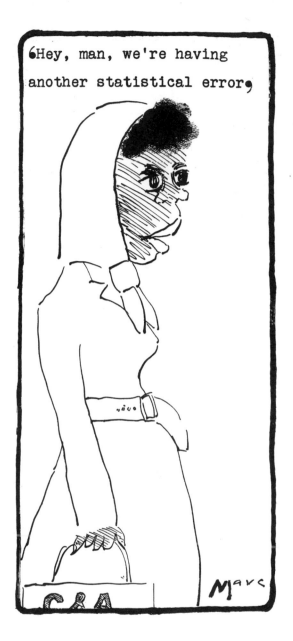

January 1976

January 1976

February 1976

Unpublished
February 1976

February 1976

March 1976

March 1976

March 1976

April 1976

April 1976

76

April 1976

Norman Scott: Newton charged
May 1976

June 1976

June 1976

June 1976

The Entebbe raid
July 1976

August 1976

August 1976

September 1976

Labour Party conference
September 1976

October 1976

November 1976

Police sell confiscated pornography
November 1976

December 1976

December 1976

'The trouble with the Royals today is that they have no incentive'

January 1977

January 1977

February 1977

March 1977

Dollar-forger charged
April 1977

May 1977

May 1977

June 1977

June 1977

FREE
UGANDA

June 1977

Driberg's memoirs published
June 1977

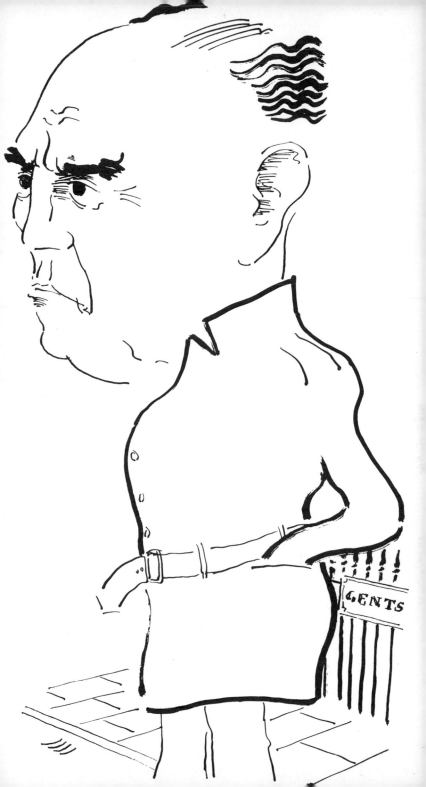

July 1977

July 1977

September 1977

September 1977

Paul Johnson and Hugh Thomas
leave Labour Party
October 1977

November 1977

December 1977

December 1977

December 1977

February 1978

February 1978

February 1978

February 1978

February 1978

February 1978

March 1978

April 1978